How a Book is Made

 Emma Lynch

Heinemann Educational Publishers
Halley Court, Jordan Hill, Oxford OX2 8EJ
a division of Reed Educational & Professional Publishing Limited

Heinemann is a registered trademark of Reed Educational & Professional Publishing Limited

OXFORD   MELBOURNE   AUCKLAND
JOHANNESBURG   BLANTYRE   GABORONE
IBADAN   PORTSMOUTH (NH) USA   CHICAGO

First published 1998

07
11

British Library Cataloguing in Publication Data
A catalogue record for this book is available from the British Library.

ISBN 978 0 435096 53 3   *How a Book is Made* single copy

ISBN 978 0 435096 54 0   *How a Book is Made* 6 copy pack

Designed by Oxprint Design
Printed and bound in China by China Translation & Printing Services Ltd.

Acknowledgements
All photographs by Trevor Clifford

Contents

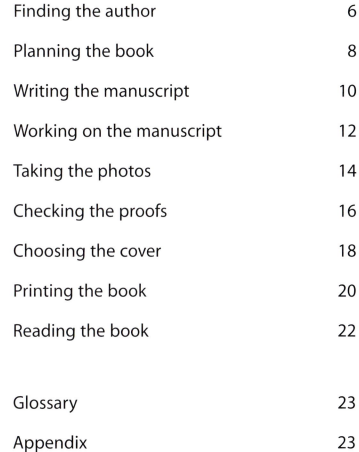

How is a book made?

31 August 1998

Dear Reader

How a Book is Made

Halley Court
Jordan Hill
Oxford OX2 8EJ UK

Telephone +44 (0)1865 311366
Fax +44 (0)1865 314140
URL http://www.heinemann.co.uk
e-mail reed.educational@bhein.rel.co.uk
Direct Line

There are billions of books in the world, but do you know how a book is made? Some people plan the books, some people write them and others make them.

This book explains how a book is made – from the first idea to the finished product. It contains letters written by some of the people involved. The letters show how useful it is to write to people to share ideas and find out their opinions. The letters are different. Sometimes they are long and **formal**; sometimes they are short and chatty. It all depends on why the people are writing to each other and how well they know each other.

I hope you enjoy the book.

Yours sincerely

Kath Donovan

Kath Donovan
Publisher

Heinemann Educational
A Division of Reed Educational
& Professional Publishing Limited

Registered Office
25 Victoria Street,
London SW1H 0EX

Registered in England 3099304
A member of sb.

What happens first?

Kath Donovan works at Heinemann Publishers. She wants to publish a new non-fiction book for 7–8 year-olds. She has decided it will be about making a book, and she wants it to be interesting as well as informative. First, she thinks about what should be included in the book, and who could write it.

Finding the author

Once Kath has thought of an author for the book, she writes to ask if she would like to write it. She does not know the author very well, so she writes a **formal** letter to her.

> A formal letter starts with the sender's address, the date and the name and address of the person it is being sent to.

> The person who is being written to is not called by their first name. Instead, their surname and title (Ms, Mr, Mrs, Miss, etc.) are used. If their name is not known, 'Dear Sir or Madam' is used.

Heinemann

Halley Court
Jordan Hill
Oxford OX2 8EJ UK

Telephone +44 (0)1865 311366
Fax +44 (0)1865 314140
URL http://www.heinemann.co.uk
e-mail reed.educational@bhein.rcl.co.uk
Direct Line

30 January 1998

Ms Emma Lynch
4 Duke Street
Rosemount Estate
LEEDS
LS23 1PZ

Dear Ms Lynch

How a Book is Made

I am currently publishing a new series of non-fiction books for Heinemann Publishers, and I am writing to ask if you would like to be one of the authors.

The book will be for 7–8 year olds and will explain how a book is made. As you have a great deal of experience in this area, I hope you will think about my suggestion.

I look forward to hearing from you.

Yours sincerely

Kath Donovan

Kath Donovan
Publisher

> The letter ends with the name and job title of the sender.

Heinemann Educational
A Division

A bright idea

Emma is very pleased to get Kath's letter. She writes back straightaway.

If your letter begins with 'Dear Sir or Madam', you end the letter with the words 'Yours faithfully' and then write your full name, as well as signing the letter. If you know the name of the person you are writing to, you end the letter 'Yours sincerely', like Emma did, and then write your full name, as well as signing the letter.

Emma Lynch
4 DUKE STREET ROSEMOUNT ESTATE LEEDS LS23 1PZ

1 February 1998

Ms Kath Donovan
Heinemann Publishers
Halley Court
Jordan Hill
OXFORD
OX2 8EJ

Dear Ms Donovan

How a Book is Made

Thank you for your letter of 30 January. I am very interested in the idea and I would like to write the book.

Perhaps we could use the making of this book to explain the publishing **process**. How about including some of the letters we write? I think this would help children to understand the part that letters play in the whole process.

I am in Oxford next week. Why don't we meet then to discuss the book?

I look forward to meeting you.

Yours sincerely

Emma Lynch.

Emma Lynch

Planning the book

Kath and Emma meet. They agree that Emma will write the book. Emma is introduced to some of the people who will work on the book with her. She is shown a plan of how the book will be made and who will do what, and is given a contract and a schedule.

HEINEMANN PUBLISHERS

This agreement is made on 10 February 1998

between

1. Heinemann Publishers of Halley Court, Jordan Hill, Oxford, OX2 8EJ, a division of Reed Educational & Professional Publishing Limited ('the Publisher')

and

2. Emma Lynch of 4 Duke Street, Rosemount Estate, Leeds, LS23 1PZ ('the Author')

DEFINITIONS

In this agreement:

1. 'The work' shall mean the book provisionally known as *How a Book is Made* for the Publisher's Literacy World non-fiction series.

2. 'Delivery date' shall mean the final manuscript delivery date set out in the schedule or another date agreed in writing by the Publisher.

3. 'Schedule' sh... of this agreem...

A contract is a letter of agreement. This contract agrees that if Emma writes the book, Kath will pay her and publish it.

Kath wants to publish her new book in September, so she plans a schedule. A schedule tells everyone when every job on the book needs to happen. If any stage runs late, the book may not be published on time.

How a Book is Made

Author: Emma Lynch
Stage: 1

ISBN: 0 435 09653 2
Extent: 24pp

	Plan	Revised	Actual
Handover to designer	12/03/98		
First proofs to Heinemann	01/04/98		
First proofs to author / adviser	01/04/98		
Comments on first proofs back to designer	09/04/98		
Second proofs to Heinemann	20/04/98		
Comments on second proofs back to designer	27/04/98		
Third proofs to Heinemann	05/05/98		
Comments on third proofs back to designer	08/05/98		
Colour proofs to Heinemann	22/05/98		
Film to Heinemann	29/05/98		
Film to printer	03/06/98		

How a book is made

The publisher plans a new book.

⬇

Finding the author

The publisher asks an author to write the book by a certain date and in a certain way.

⬇

Working on the manuscript

The author sends a *first draft* of the *manuscript* to the publisher. The publisher may ask for changes to the manuscript. The author makes changes and sends a *final draft* to the publisher. An editor corrects any mistakes. A designer plans how the book will look and makes it into *proofs.*

⬇

Taking the photos

A picture researcher finds photos for the book, or uses a photographer to take special photos.

⬇

Checking the proofs

Everyone checks the proofs very carefully to make sure they are right. They do this several times.

⬇

Choosing the cover

The designer has lots of ideas for the book cover. The best cover idea is chosen.

⬇

Printing the book

The proofs are made into film and then sent to the printer. Thousands of copies of the book are printed and stored in a warehouse.

⬇

Reading the book

Schools order the book and, at last, the book is sent to you, the reader!

Writing the manuscript

Now Emma writes a **manuscript**. She tries to do exactly what Kath wants. Once it is finished, she sends the **first draft** to Kath, who reads the manuscript and also sends it to an adviser to read.

HEINEMANN

With Compliments

Gill,

Here's the 'How a Book is Made' manuscript. I've had a quick look at it and it seems fine. I'll give you a ring next week when we've both had a chance to read it properly.

Best wishes,

Kath

Heinemann Educational Publishers
Halley Court
Jordan Hill
Oxford OX2 8EJ
UK

Telephone +44 (0)1865 311366
Telex 837292 HEBOXF G
Fax +44 (0)1865 310043

A member of the Reed Elsevier plc group

Page 4

\<Heading\> **How is a book made?**

Mock-up 1: Letter from Kath to reader

\<Heinemann headed paper\>

31 August 1998

Dear Reader,

How a Book is Made

There are billions of books in the world, but do you know how a book is made? Some people plan the books, some write them and others make them.

This book explains how a book is made – from the first idea to the finished product. It contains letters written by some of the people involved. The letters show how useful it is to write to people to share ideas and find out their opinions. The letters vary. Sometimes they are long and formal; sometimes they are short and chatty. It all depends on why the people are writing to each other and how well they know each other.

Making changes

Kath and Gill read the manuscript. They are pleased with it, but feel that a few changes are needed. They talk about the changes, then Kath writes to Emma.

2 March 1998

Ms Emma Lynch
4 Duke Street
Rosemount Estate
LEEDS
LS23 1PZ

Dear Emma

How a Book Is Made

I hope you're well and that you enjoyed the karate course. What a great way to forget about work!

I have read your manuscript and I have also had comments on it from an adviser. It's good news – we really like the manuscript. It is well written and the ideas flow well. You will need to make a few changes, though. I think some of the words you use are too difficult and in some places there are too many words on the page.

I've made a list of things you need to look at and have sent it with this letter. Please will you make these changes to your manuscript? Can you do this by next week?

Thank you for all the work you're doing. It's going to be a great book!

Best wishes.

Yours sincerely

Kath

Kath Donovan
Publisher

> Kath knows Emma now, so she sends her an informal letter. She still puts the date, address, Emma's full name and title at the top of the letter and her own at the bottom, but she now uses first names in the letter. The style of the letter is chatty and friendly.

Heinemann Educational
A Division of Reed Educational
& Professional Publishing Limited

Registered Office
25 Victoria Street,
London SW1H 0EX

Registered in England 3099304

A member of the Reed Elsevier plc group

Emma finds Kath's comments very helpful. She makes changes to her manuscript and sends off the **final draft**.

Working on the manuscript

Now Kath gives the **manuscript** to Julie, the editor. Julie makes a few changes to the manuscript. She corrects any mistakes and makes sure that it is ready to go to the designer.

Julie makes special marks on the manuscript. They are instructions about how the book should be corrected. These marks are explained in the appendix on page 23.

Page 15

Choosing the photos

The photographer takes many photos. sally chooses the best ones for each page of the book. When they are ready they are sent to the design studio so that they can

Page 16

Checking the proofs

Proofs have to be carefully ch
on the book to make sure tha
and work well together. They
times. There are first, second
white. Finally there are colour
book is printed. The proofing
months.

<Caption>

First proofs usually have some mistakes in them. Corre
marked on the proofs using signs like the ones that we
manuscript (see appendix on page 23).

MEMO

To: Jon Hicks   **Re:** How a Book is Made
From: Julie McCulloch   **Date:** 12 March 1998

Jon

This is one you'll like – it's a book about making a book! Let's hope it all runs smoothly (as if!).

Here is the manuscript on computer disk and on paper, together with a list of photos. The photos will be ready at the end of this week, so I'll pass them on then.

Let me know if you have any questions about the manuscript. I'm looking forward to seeing **proofs** on 1 April.

Thanks. *Julie*

Julie sends a memo to Jon, the designer. A memo is a short letter to one or more people in the same company. This means that Julie does not need to write Jon's address on the memo and she can use first names.

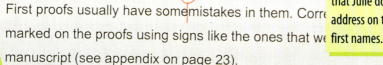

Designing the book

Jon plans a design and layout for the book. When he is happy with it, he sends the manuscript and his design to a design studio. They will follow his ideas and make the book into proofs.

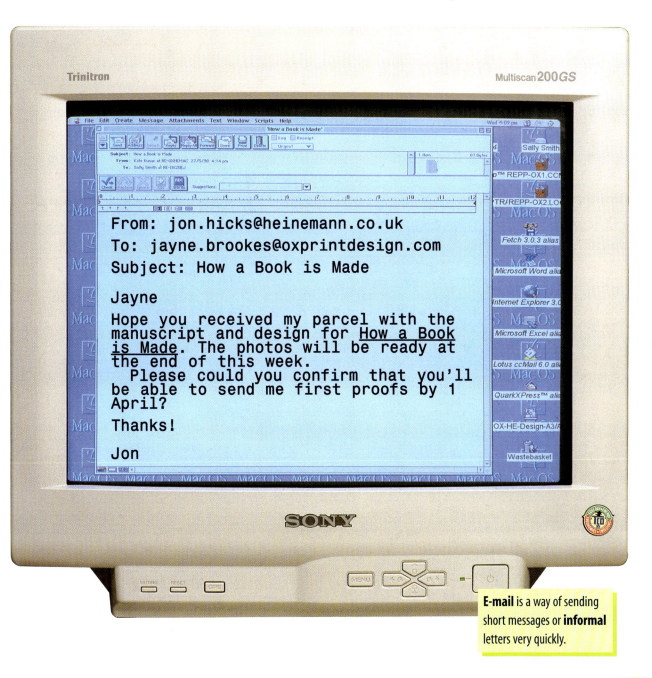

From: jon.hicks@heinemann.co.uk
To: jayne.brookes@oxprintdesign.com
Subject: How a Book is Made

Jayne

Hope you received my parcel with the manuscript and design for How a Book is Made. The photos will be ready at the end of this week.
   Please could you confirm that you'll be able to send me first proofs by 1 April?

Thanks!

Jon

E-mail is a way of sending short messages or **informal** letters very quickly.

Taking the photos

While Julie works on the words, Sally, the picture researcher, thinks about photos for the book. For some books, Sally borrows photos from a special photo library. For this book, though, she decides to hire a photographer.

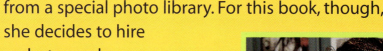

Sally plans the photoshoot. She works out who and what needs to be in each photo and tells the photographer what she needs.

Choosing the photos

The photographer takes many photos. Sally chooses the best ones for each page of the book. When they are ready they are sent to the design studio so that they can be included in the **proofs**.

Checking the proofs

Proofs have to be checked carefully by everyone who works on the book to make sure that the words and pictures make sense and work well together. They are corrected and changed several times. There are first, second and third proofs, which are black and white. Finally there are colour proofs. This is the last stage before the book is printed. The proofing **process** may last for several months.

First proofs usually have some mistakes in them. Corrections are marked on the proofs using special marks like the ones that were put on the manuscript (see appendix on page 23).

Problems!

Julie is worried because Emma has not sent her first proofs back. She sends a **fax**.

14 April 1998

Ms Emma Lynch
4 Duke Street
Rosemount Estate
LEEDS
LS23 1PZ

Halley Court
Jordan Hill
Oxford ox2 8ej UK

Telephone +44 (0)1865 311366
Fax +44 (0)1865 314140
URL http://www.heinemann.co.uk
e-mail reed.educational@bhein.rel.co.uk
Direct Line

Fax: 0113 233 1898

Dear Emma

How a Book is Made

I've been trying to talk to you for a week now because I'm worried about the book.

You said you would send me your first proofs back, with captions for the photos, a week ago. The book is now running late and we might not be able to publish it in September, which will let a lot of people down.

Please ring me and let me know what is happening. I hope everything is OK.

Yours sincerely

Julie

Julie McCulloch
Editor

> Sometimes you have to write a letter to complain, which can be difficult. Julie writes a polite, **informal** letter to Emma, and faxes it to her.

Panasonic

Emma rings Julie the next day. She went on holiday and forgot to post her proofs before she went! She apologises to Julie and promises to post them immediately.

Choosing the cover

While the inside of the book is being made, a lot of time is spent planning a cover. The designer has many ideas, but the best cover is one that is eye-catching, clear to read and shows what the book is about. A meeting is held to choose the cover.

MINUTES OF COVERS MEETING

To:
Kath Donovan
Julie McCulloch
Jon Hicks
Sally Smith

From: Rod Smith

Date: 15 April 1998

How a Book is Made

- Cover A does not tell us what the book is about.
- Cover B is not very clear. It is too hard to read the title.
- Cover C is great. It's fun, young, clear and makes you want to read it. Use this one!

Testing

Books are often tried out in schools before they are finished. This is called trialling. It is done in order to check whether there are any problems with the book before it is printed.

Printing the book

Finally, the **proofs** are made into film. The printer prints thousands of copies of the book from the film onto paper (rather like the way photos are printed from negatives). At the same time, a team of salespeople visits schools to tell teachers about the book.

The books are kept in a warehouse until people buy them.

Publication

At last the book is finished and sent to schools. Kath is very pleased with it. She writes to Emma to congratulate her and to say thank you.

Heinemann

Halley Court
Jordan Hill
Oxford ox2 8EJ UK

Telephone +44 (0)1865 311366
Fax +44 (0)1865 314140
URL http://www.heinemann.co.uk
e-mail reed.educational@bhein.rel.co.uk

Direct Line

1 September 1998

Ms Emma Lynch
4 Duke Street
Rosemount Estate
Leeds
LS23 1PZ

Dear Emma

How a Book Is Made

Here they are – six free copies of your book! Congratulations! I think it is wonderful and I'm sure that children will really enjoy reading it.

Thank you for all your hard work.

I look forward to working with you again.

Best wishes.

Yours sincerely

Kath

Kath Donovan
Publisher

Heinemann Educational
A Division of Reed Educational
& Professional Publishing Limited

Registered Office
25 Victoria Street,
London SW1H 0EX

Registered in England 3099304

A member of the Reed Elsevier plc group

Reading the book

Kath was right. Children and teachers really like the book. Some children want to show what they have learned from the book, so they write a letter to the author.

Langley Primary School
New Road
Langley
Buckinghamshire
MK19 4EP

9 October 1998

Ms Emma Lynch
4 Duke Street
Rosemount Estate
LEEDS
LS23 1PZ

Dear Ms Lynch

How a Book is Made

We have just read *How a Book is Made* and we really enjoyed it. We found out how books are made and how many people help to make them.

We liked all the different kinds of letters. Our favourite part was when the photographer took a horrible photo of Kath and it was in the book!

Yours sincerely

Rebecca
Mukesh Emma David Ingrid
Danny NATASHA
Paul Shamina
Monica

Class 3A
Langley Primary School

Glossary

e-mail   a message that people send from computer screen to computer screen, down a telephone line

fax   an urgent message that is sent by fax machine, down a telephone line. It reaches another fax machine in minutes and prints out as a letter.

formal   polite and following certain rules. You write a formal letter to people you do not know well.

informal   casual or familiar. You send an informal letter to someone you know.

manuscript   the author's words before they are printed

first draft   the first version of a book that the author writes

final draft   the version of a book that is printed, when the author has made changes to it

process   the way something is done or made

proofs   pages that show how a book will look. They are made before the book is printed, so it can be checked for mistakes.

Appendix

These are some of the special marks that are put on manuscripts and proofs to show changes that need to be made. They are a bit like a code.

Delete a letter or letters		Make this word bold type
Insert a word or letter		Make this a capital letter
Swop these words around		Insert a space here
Close the gap between letters or words		Delete a letter and close the gap
Join these paragraphs		Insert a hyphen

Index